Wilder Mississippi

Mississippi is a landscape,

a riverscape, a seascape.

But beyond its topography lies another

Mississippi. A Mississippi of wild things

and wild places, an elusive Eden that

beckons to the outdoorsman in each of us.

This wilder Mississippi is untamed,

unspoiled, and unmapped.

This wilder Mississippi is a heartscape.

WHITE-TAILED DEER IN LEAVES

Wilder Mississippi

STEPHEN KIRKPATRICK

WRITTEN BY

MARLO CARTER KIRKPATRICK

VULTURES IN TREE

Film

Mention "Mississippi," and my mind, like my cameras, focuses on the outdoors.
The state's wilder side calls, inviting me to stir my spirit with a visit, and maybe –
just maybe – to capture a memorable image or two while I'm there.

Photographing wild things and wild places is always a challenge.
Once you step off the city streets, any illusion of control is quickly dispelled.
As a photographer dedicated solely to nature and wildlife, I'm often frustrated
by the infinite, unpredictable, uncontrollable obstacles waiting to disrupt
every photographic opportunity. I'm constantly reminded
that in wildlife photography, *patience* is as important a tool as film.

But sometimes, it all comes together. There it is – that rare image,
that magical moment when film and fantasy merge. And more often than not,
no matter how much planning was involved, it's a completely serendipitous event.
A reminder that while God never intended certain things and places to be tamed,
He graciously allows us a glimpse of them every once in a while.

It's my pleasure to share the results of that patience, serendipity,
and heavenly benevolence in the following pages. And in this exhibition
of mayflies and magnolias, bobcats and bayous, ducks and dogwoods,
I hope you'll also see a passion.

An enthusiastic passion for a wilder Mississippi.

Fantasy

STEPHEN KIRKPATRICK

SEPTEMBER 2001

Carolina Chickadee in Redbud

PREVIOUS PAGE: Mayapple on Hillside

Contents

Sweetgum Tree (fall, winter, spring, & summer)

Heart Song

The heavy perfume of a magnolia in bloom.

The majestic river that gave the state its name.

Towering pines and patriarchal live oaks, cheerful songbirds,

and the wobbly steps of a newborn fawn.

It's shamefully easy to take some of Mississippi's

most wondrous wilderness gifts for granted. Encountered with

delightful frequency, these Mississippi icons seem to have lost their wild flavor

and become almost commonplace, perhaps even a bit cliché.

But a thing becomes cliché only because it so perfectly captures

the essence of a place. Only when a single image of that animal, tree, or scene

tells a familiar story. Only when the briefest glimpse

or faintest suggestion instantly strikes a chord within the heart.

Foxtail & Dew at Sunrise

CHAMPION LIVE OAK NEAR COAST

MISSISSIPPI SANDHILL CRANES IN FLIGHT

Brown Pelicans at Sunset near Horn Island

FALL COLOR

GREAT BLUE HERONS

Heart Song

DOE NURSING FAWN IN KUDZU

TREES & LANDSCAPE NEAR DE KALB

Heart Song

DOGWOODS & PINES

Heart Song

Borne on the Wind

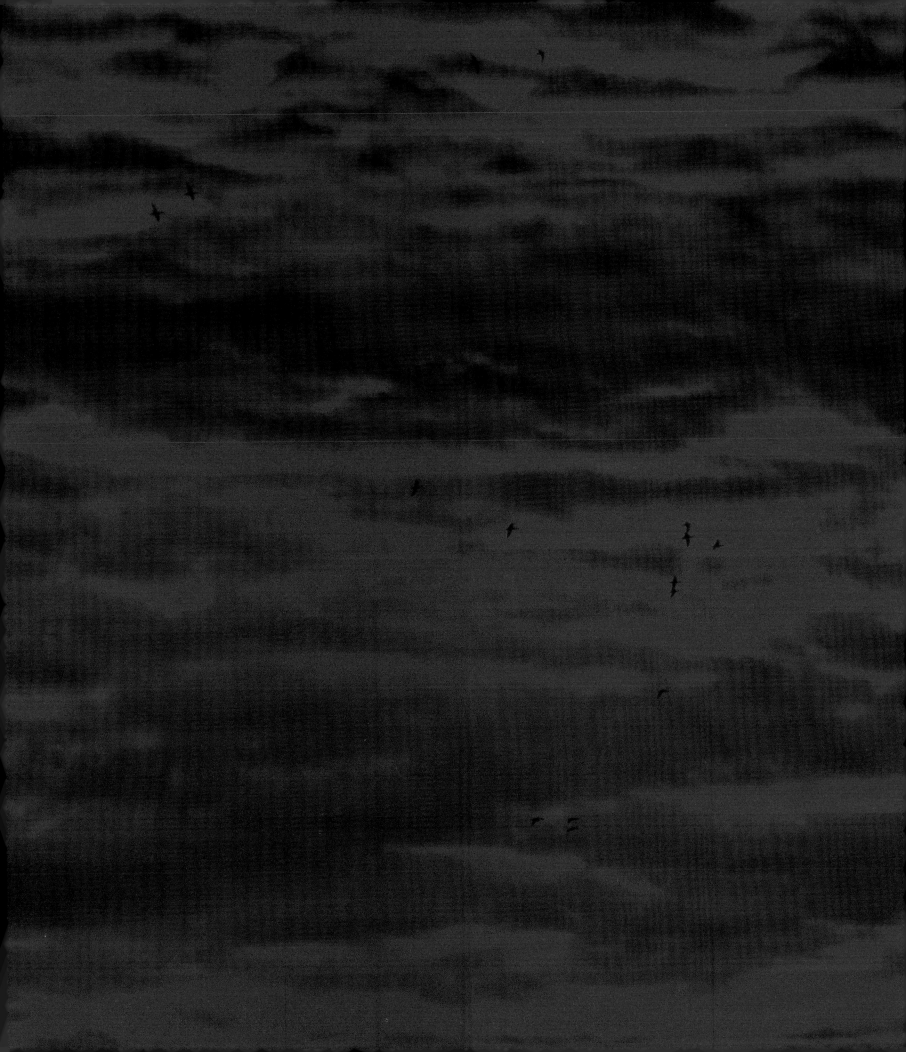

Bound to the land, they are clumsy and awkward,

off-balance fowl punctuating their ungainly waddles with indignant quacks.

But soaring in the lofty freedom of the Mississippi Flyway,

they are nothing short of inspirational. Wheeling amid the wind-torn clouds

or breaking through the early morning fog, they speak

of distant views, unfettered freedom, possibilities as limitless as the heavens.

Watching them fly, it's little wonder that the rush of whistling wings

can bring a grown, camouflage-clad man to tears.

Witness the glorious takeoff, the skillful navigation, and the sheer,

aerodynamic grace, and the Creator's intention is unmistakably clear.

Ducks are not only borne on the wind,

but born for the wind.

MALLARDS COMING INTO FLOODED TIMBER

BLUE-WINGED TEAL TAKING OFF

SHOVELERS AT DUSK

MALLARD LANDING IN FLOODED TIMBER

MALLARDS AT DAWN

In Secret Places

Mississippi boasts no purple mountain majesties,

no panoramic desert expanses, no jagged cliffs tumbling to the sea.

Instead, Mississippi's wilderness is a place of subtle splendor

and understated charm, of quiet beauty the casual observer might miss.

In this land of pathless woods, secluded shores, and unmarked waysides,

nature shuns the dramatic in favor of a more intimate encounter.

Wilder Mississippi promises a confidential adventure,

like being let in on a wonderful secret.

Here, nature's precious gems are carefully tucked away,

a hidden reward for those willing to seek them out.

A wilderness experience here isn't simply given, but earned –

and ultimately proves more rewarding for the effort.

MARBLED SALAMANDER & WHITE VIOLETS

GREEN LYNX SPIDER ON BLAZING STAR

In Secret Places

YELLOW UNICORN ENTOLOMA

BOBCAT LOOKING FOR TURKEY

Cottontail Rabbit

Least Bittern in Cattails

Quiet Time

Mississippi's wildest places possess its greatest peace.

The state's sheltering forests and tranquil marshes

are natural sanctuaries, made for moments of quiet reflection.

In these pristine places, the perils and pace of urban life

are distant memories, and pleasures and problems alike

are reduced to a simpler essence.

A retreat to these unspoiled spaces stirs the senses,

yet soothes the soul. For while these wild havens are blessed

with a calming sense of solitude, we know we're never truly alone here.

The state's verdant cathedrals resound not only

with the quiet peace of Mississippi,

but with the awesome presence of its Maker.

REFLECTIONS

DEER BEFORE DAWN IN BAYOU PIERRE

RIVER OTTER RESTING

Black Cherry after Rain

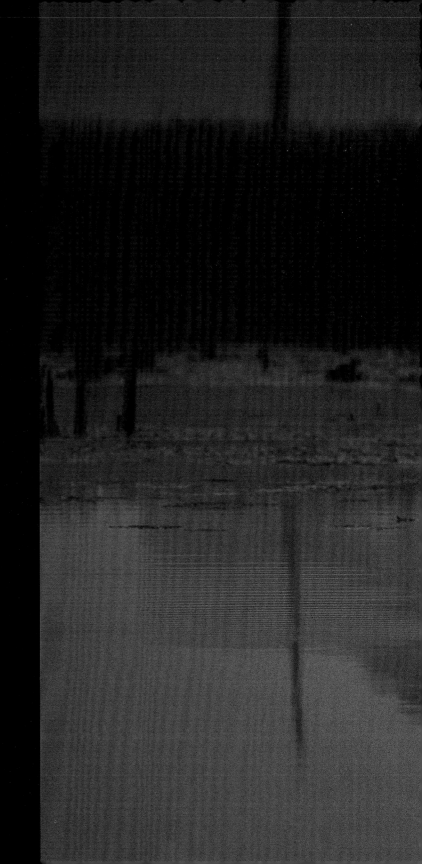

WOOD DUCKS AT DAWN

Living Waters

Mississippi's rivers, marshes, lakes, and seas brim with life.

Feeding, drinking, bathing, or simply splashing in for the pure, wet joy of it,

Mississippi's wild inhabitants form a brilliant, living mural

that transcends mere watercolors.

Of course, it comes as no great revelation that wildlife is often found

near life-sustaining water. But what may not be so fully appreciated

is the power of those same waters to sustain the human soul.

There is renewal in a creek's crystal currents, refreshment in the gulf's

wind-whipped waves, restoration in a river's endless ripples. Viewed from

the water's edge, life seems more immediate, more vital, more abundant.

Overflowing with life, Mississippi's wild waters

replenish the wild spirit in each of us.

HORSESHOE CRAB ON COAST

FRAGRANT WATER LILY

WOOD DUCK FAMILY

BULLFROG & BULLHEAD LILY

HOODED MERGANSER STRETCHING

CYPRESS KNEES AT SUNRISE

GREAT EGRET EATING BASS

Nature's Palette

It comes in splashy, showy rainbows, vibrant murals painted

across the rain-dulled sky. It's borne on the delicate wings of butterflies

and songbirds, tiny swatches that shimmer in the sunshine.

It's found in the born-again glory of spring blossoms

and in explosive displays of fall foliage too brilliant to be ignored.

It is color. Vivid, kaleidoscopic color all the more spectacular

because it is natural, and nature isn't limited to a mere sixty-four crayolas.

In addition to every hue and shade mixed by the Creator,

nature's palette includes rain, fog, sunshine, and subtle variations of light

capable of transforming an unassuming scene into an iridescent masterpiece.

Nature's palette is limitless, her canvas is the wilderness,

and her gallery is all of Mississippi.

SUMAC & GOLDENROD

FALL COLOR & PINES

QUARTER MOONRISE AT DAWN

BROWN SNAKE ON LEAF

Field Notes

One moment, the wilderness is empty. Then suddenly, soundlessly, they materialize.

They stand with cupped ears and raised flags, their mahogany coats

a natural velvet, their sable eyes liquid, and for the briefest moment, meeting your own.

And, when the story is later recited, at least one pair of enormous, graceful

antlers casts long shadows in the early morning light.

The gobbler prefers to announce his appearance, voicing his distinctive call,

fanning his regal feathers, brandishing his lengthy spurs, and waggling his venerable

beard in a display that is anything but subtle. But while he seems

completely enthralled with his own performance, he's keenly aware of his surroundings.

Blink first, and the encounter is over.

A glimpse of these noble animals makes the eyes widen, the heart pound, the breath

catch in our throats. They keep us ever-hopeful, ever-watchful, searching for the

massive rack of the phantom buck or listening for the distant call of the wily old tom.

Constantly seeking the elusive wildlife that haunts not only Mississippi's fields

and woodlands, but our own imagination.

BUCK & FAWN IN FIELD

EASTERN WILD TURKEYS STRUTTING

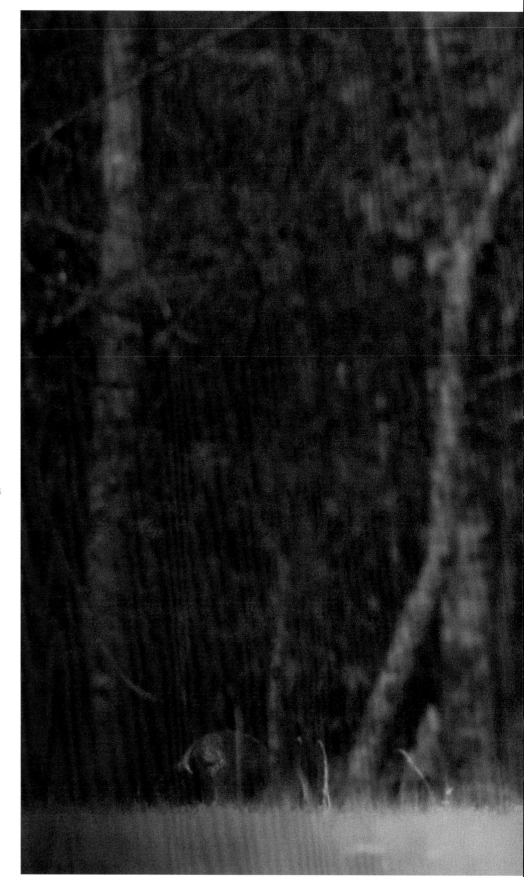

BUCK FOLLOWING DOE,
LATE AFTERNOON

DEER SMELLING LICHEN

Mind's Eye

Wilder Mississippi is more than geography or biology, more than scenery or wildlife.

Above all else, wilder Mississippi is a personal encounter.

Wilder Mississippi is a feeling that you've traveled farther, seen and

experienced more than just another side of a place you thought you knew.

It's being touched by things you never expected, and by things

you've always taken for granted. And it's learning that you can't make

the journey there without returning somehow different.

Wilder Mississippi is a place that's timeless, yet ever-changing.

It's a place you've yet to explore, as familiar as your own backyard.

A place to get lost in, and a place to find yourself.

Wilder Mississippi is a vision that lingers in your own mind's eye,

a passion that lives in your heart.

ELEPHANT STAG BEETLE

DEW COVERED BUTTERFLY, SPIDER & WEB

HICKORY LEAVES IN CYPRESS SWAMP

MOCKINGBIRD EATING ANOLE

OWENS CREEK WATERFALL

HUMMINGBIRD IN TRUMPET CREEPER

GREEN HERON AT SUNRISE

BIG BAYOU BLACK AT SUNRISE

TUPELO SUNRISE

BROWN PELICAN DIVING AT SUNSET

Wilder Mississippi

Thy Marvelous Works
102 Proprietor's Point
Madison, MS 39110

www.kirkpatrickwildlife.com

ISBN # 0-9619353-5-9

Library of Congress Control Number: 2001126374

First Edition

Printer:
Friesens
Canada

Prepress & Scanning:
Photo Images
Flowood, MS

Designer:
Heidi Flynn Allen, Flynn Design
Jackson, MS

Proofreader:
Sissy Yerger
Clinton, MS

"This Is It!"

PEOPLE OFTEN SAY TO ME, "YOU MUST BE A VERY PATIENT PERSON."

BUT THAT'S ONLY TRUE PART OF THE TIME. IN THE FIELD OR IN A BLIND,
I HAVE A MOUNTAIN OF PATIENCE. BUT WAITING FOR THE FILM TO COME BACK,
I CAN'T CLAIM EVEN A DUSTING OF IT.

IT'S HARD TO DESCRIBE THE PHYSICAL ANXIETY I EXPERIENCE WAITING
FOR THOSE PRECIOUS SLIDES TO RETURN FROM THE LAB. MANY TIMES, THE RESULTS
CONFIRM MY WORST FEARS. IT REALLY *DIDN'T* HAPPEN AS I'D ENVISIONED IT.

BUT EVERY ONCE IN AWHILE, IT DOES.

THE IMAGES DESCRIBED HERE REPRESENT A FEW OF THOSE "FILM AND FANTASY" MOMENTS,
WHEN THE DEFINITIVE IMAGE I'D IMAGINED ACTUALLY SHOWED UP ON THE SLIDE.
THESE 12 SHOTS WERE THE FIRST IMAGES SELECTED FOR *WILDER MISSISSIPPI*,
SET ASIDE BEFORE HUNDREDS OF OTHERS WERE EVEN CONSIDERED.

I GUESS YOU COULD SAY THEY WERE CHOSEN THE MOMENT I LOOKED
THROUGH THE LENS AND WHISPERED, "THIS IS IT!"

PURPLE GALLINULE IN FLIGHT (COVER)
JUNE 1999, 400MM, 1/125@F3.5

I was working in my familiar "frog's eye view" style, following a purple gallinule as it fed among the lilies. I'd tried to get a great shot of one of these colorful birds in flight for years, but never succeeded in capturing it. Gallinules rarely fly, and predicting the moment of takeoff is next to impossible.

As this gallinule hopped from lily pad to lily pad, I prepared for it to take flight, at the same time praying it would wait long enough for the still-rising sun to bathe its iridescent feathers in golden morning light.

Suddenly and with a squawk, the gallinule took off. I followed, focused, and captured a single shot. I worked for another two hours that morning, but that solitary shot never left my mind. If only this time....

PEARLY CRESCENTSPOT AND DEW (PAGE 7)
SEPTEMBER 1999, 105MM MACRO, 2 SEC.@F22

I've spent many cool, foggy mornings roaming a field near my home, searching for subjects covered in dew. The time I spend there is always invigorating, but every now and then I find something truly special.

On this particular morning, I spotted the tiny (less than an inch tall), sparkling shape of a familiar friend, the pearly crescentspot. While I had shot this jewel of a butterfly many times, its presentation atop the delicate purple vervain made for a special composition. I knew this was it.

At 1:1, focus was critical. The setting was extremely fragile – the slightest disturbance or faintest breeze, and the entire scene would be destroyed. And even with perfect focus and no hint of movement, the lighting would have to be ideal. Getting it right took over an hour.

An observer may have thought I was talking to myself as I shot that morning; I was actually repeating over and over, "Thank you, Lord."

MISSISSIPPI RIVER IN FOGGY SUNRISE (PAGE 16)
OCTOBER 1995, 24MM, 1/4@F22

I've shot the Mississippi River on many occasions, seldom to my satisfaction. One cold October morning, my good friends Bobby McCain and the late Charlie Shorter and I headed to the river to shoot footage for a video.

When we reached the riverbank, I couldn't believe my eyes. The definitive Mississippi River shot I'd seen in my mind's eye – wide, winding, mysterious – stretched before me.

As I composed the shot, the rising sun emerged from the fog, completing the scene. My heart was pounding. The image I'd dreamed of had finally come, a gift from above.

MALLARDS COMING INTO FLOODED TIMBER (PAGE 44)
DECEMBER 1989, 24MM, 1/125@F2.8

Waist-deep in flooded timber, I peered up through dark woods into the early morning sky, and thought my heart would explode with excitement.

Three to four thousand mallards "fell" on top of me through a tight corridor in the trees. The deafening sound of their chatter and the crash of their wings upon the tree limbs only added to the thrill of the moment.

The only way to capture any of it on film was through a wide-angle lens. It's hard to imagine how close the ducks actually were – some even splashed water on me as they crashed into the surface. It was definitely a you-had-to-be-there moment.

MARBLED SALAMANDER AND WHITE VIOLETS (PAGE 59)
MARCH 1998, 105MM MACRO, 4 SEC.@F22

In the lifeless winter woods, spring was still only a dream. A rare warm day found me searching for anything that would hasten that dream along. The sun was setting as I turned over one last log.

There it was – a familiar black-and-white patterned salamander. I noticed the white violets blooming in the moss alongside the little amphibian, and decided that even though the lighting was flat, it was worth at least one shot.

Then the last rays of sunlight beamed through the leafless trees, giving life to the eyes of my formerly unassuming subject. Photography really *is* the art of discovery!

SCAUP DIVING IN GULF (PAGE 86)
MARCH 1995, 400 MM W/1.4 TC, 1/250@4.9

Working on the coast one spring, I spotted a group of ducks in the distance out from the shore. I watched them for over an hour as they swam, slept, and preened. Thinking they might take off, I sat down in the cool water near the shoreline, shoving my tripod deep into the sand to get a low angle of view. Instead, the ducks swam toward me, coming surprisingly close as they fed beneath the water's surface.

Looking for that special moment, I shot image after image as they dove and surfaced. The timing was split-second. I would not know for days whether I'd managed to capture my vision – the essence of diving ducks!

WATER MOCCASIN IN DUCKWEED (PAGE 92)
JUNE 1999, 400MM, 1/30@3.5

I was neck-deep in duckweed when the cameraman yelled, "Snake!"

When I looked up, he was trembling. A California videographer here to film my frog's eye view technique for the TV show "Wild Things," he'd never set foot in a southern swamp before, much less with an aggressive, poisonous snake quite literally underfoot. As if on cue, the cottonmouth slid into the dark water and swam directly toward me while the producer screamed, "Roll film! Roll film!"

I was unprepared – after all, I was supposed to be the *subject* of this shoot! Instead, I found myself shooting with the big lens hand-held. Considering the slow shutter speed, a usable image was probably a dream.

I shot seven frames before the snake swam out of sight. Six were blurry. The seventh is still giving the videographer nightmares.

WOOD DUCKS, ADULT AND IMMATURE (PAGE 110)
JUNE 2000, 400MM, 1/250@F3.5

I waded chest-deep through the swamp for hours, my laborious movement dictated by shallow channels beneath the surface. I slowly rounded a thick covering of lotus plants and spotted an adult wood duck sleeping on a log. A second duck, this one an immature male, swam in the lilies before me. He saw my floating blind and stopped. I lowered my face and eyes behind the camera until my chin touched the water.

Barely shifting from this position, I shot for over an hour. The "father and son" soon became comfortable with my presence, sleeping, swimming, eating, and preening before the camera. Of the 17 frames I exposed, this shot best captured the essence of youth and maturity.

MAYFLY ON RAZORGRASS (PAGE 112)
MAY 2000, 105MM MACRO, 1/8@F11

I shot and shot and shot. I had done everything I could to document the short life span of the mayfly, but nothing I saw through the lens excited me. Then I looked down to my right, and there it was.

The rising sun backlit what seconds earlier had been just a mayfly on a piece of grass. Now, life and death were clearly represented by the two leaves. Resting upon the latter, its short life over, the mayfly appeared to pray.

BUCK AND FAWN IN FIELD (PAGE 121)
NOVEMBER 1998, 400MM W/1.4 TC, 1/30@4.9

Waiting in a small blind late on an overcast day, I watched as two fawns played together at the edge of a field. Watching was all I could do – the fawns were moving too much in the low light for me to capture any of their antics on film. Suddenly, one of the fawns darted into the field. A buck appeared, and the nervous fawn walked toward him, moving closer and closer as the big buck fed.

Words cannot describe my frustration – I had never seen this behavior before, but still didn't have enough light to capture it on film. I was at 1/15 of a second. Rather than let the opportunity slip away, I decided I would underexpose at 1/30 of a second and worry about it later. I made my decision not a moment too soon. Just as the buck raised his head and looked at the fawn, I got one dark, underexposed shot. When the photo is printed it must be lightened, but at least I have a record of a moment I may never see again.

BLACK-FACED SKIMMER ON SKULLCAP (PAGE 144)
MAY 1994, 105MM MACRO, 1/4@F16

I'd been following the dragonfly from resting place to resting place for half an hour before it settled. But it wasn't the skimmer's perfect stillness that entranced me, it was the spot where it had finally chosen to rest. The lavender skullcap was a perfect complement to the skimmer's blue body. Earlier, I had been frustrated with the soft light of the overcast sky. Now, I realized it was a godsend.

BROWN PELICAN DIVING AT SUNSET (PAGE 153)
MARCH 1999, 400MM, 1/60@F3.5

The pelicans had been active all afternoon, but I wanted late evening fishing shots. As I waited for sunset, clouds formed, and soon covered the sun. I needed a fast shutter speed to stop the action, but the light was low and fading fast. When I saw that I was only at 1/60 of a second, I knew I couldn't stop the action of the diving pelican. There is, however, a fractional second at the pinnacle of its dive when the pelican hangs almost motionless.

Some decisions are made for you.

Thank You

A heartfelt thanks to those directly connected to some of
the images in *Wilder Mississippi*.

Cliff Covington, Jay Geddie, Bob Harris, Kaneaster Hodges, Ike Hopper, Charles Knight,
Monroe Mathis, Bobby McCain, Sidney Montgomery, G. F. Watts, and Kelley Williams.

The contributions of the late Howard Miller, Charlie Shorter,
and Bill Walker are also reflected in these pages.

Thanks also to several companies and organizations which contributed
to *Wilder Mississippi*, including:
ChemFirst, Inc.
Chevron, Inc.
Crow's Neck Environmental Education Center
Mississippi Department of Wildlife, Fisheries & Parks
Mississippi Museum of Natural Science
Mississippi Wildlife Federation
National Park Service
The Nature Conservancy
Tara Wildlife Management, Inc.